KU-008-446

Greatest Conquerors

Tracey Turner

EDGE FRANKLIN WATTS

LONDON · SYDNEY

First published in 2013 by
Franklin Watts
338 Euston Road
London NW1 3BH

Franklin Watts Australia
Level 17/207 Kent Street
Sydney NSW 2000

Text © Tracey Turner 2013
Design © Franklin Watts 2013

All rights reserved.

Series editor: Adrian Cole
Art direction: Peter Scoulding
Design: D R Ink
Picture research: Diana Morris

Acknowledgements:
Arclight Films: 12. Andrea Astes/istockphoto: 10.
Joseph Friedhuber/istockphoto 4. The Granger
Collection/Topfoto: 13, 17, 18, 20, 22.
Sadik Güleç/istockphoto: 19. Ralf Hettler/istockphoto: 6.
Jpa1999/istockphoto: 5. Meunierd/Shutterstock: front cover t.
NGIC/BAL: 23. Oksana/Shutterstock: front cover , back cover.
Picturepoint/Topham: 14, 21. Ria Novosti/Topfoto: 15.
Robana/The British Library Board/Topfoto: 8.
Roger-Viollet/Topfoto: 7, 16. Ullsteinbild/Topfoto: 9.
World History Archive/Topfoto: 11.

Every attempt has been made to clear copyright.
Should there be any inadvertent omission please
apply to the publisher for rectification.

A CIP catalogue record for this book
is available from the British Library.

Dewey Classification: 909
ISBN: 978 1 4451 1450 7

Printed in China

Franklin Watts is a division of Hachette
Children's Books, an Hachette UK company.
www.hachette.co.uk

Warning! This is not a normal book!

Contents

Please note: every effort has been made by the Publishers to ensure that
the websites in this book contain no inappropriate or offensive material.
However, because of the nature of the Internet, it is impossible to
guarantee that the contents of these sites will not be altered. We strongly
advise that Internet access is supervised by a responsible adult.

Ultimate 20 is not just a book where you can find out loads of facts and stats about fantastic stuff – it's also a brilliant game book!

How to play

1. Grab a copy of *Ultimate 20* – oh, you have. OK, now get your friends to grab a copy, too.

2. Each player closes their eyes and flicks to a game page. Now, open your eyes and choose one of the Ultimate 20. Decide who goes first, then that person reads out what conqueror they've chosen, plus the name of the stat. For example, this player has chosen Julius Caesar and the Army Strength stat, with an Ultimate 20 ranking of 3.

Age at death: 55	12
Length of reign 9 years	16
Army strength:	3
Terror rating:	16
Battle skill:	4
Leadership:	16

3. Now, challenge your friends to see who has the highest-ranking stat – the lower the number (from 1–20) the better your chances of winning. (1 = good, 20 = goofy.)

Player 1

Army Strength:	3

Player 2

Army Strength:	7

4. Whoever has the lowest number is the winner – nice one! If you have the same number – you've tied.

Time to flick, choose, challenge again!

(If you land on the same game page, choose the Ultimate 20 listing opposite.)

Mash it up!

If you haven't got the same *Ultimate 20* book as your friends, you can **STILL** play — Ultimate 20 Mash Up! The rules are the same as the regular game (above), so flick and choose one of your Ultimate 20 and a stat, then read them out. Each player does this. Now read out the Ultimate 20 ranking to see whose choice is the best. Can a McLaren P1 car beat a tank? Can Bobby Charlton beat a king cobra snake?

Genghis Khan

Mongolian leader Genghis Khan, or 'universal leader',
conquered an empire that became the second largest in the
history of the world. When he died in 1227, the Mongolian
Empire was vast – from Eastern Europe to Southeast Asia.

United tribes

As a boy, Genghis Khan was called Temujin. His father – the
chief of his tribe in the Gobi Desert – was killed when Temujin
was nine. He was cast out, then captured by a rival tribe, but
he escaped. Temujin quickly earned a reputation for courage
and ruthlessness. He persuaded the different Mongol
tribes to join together under his leadership.

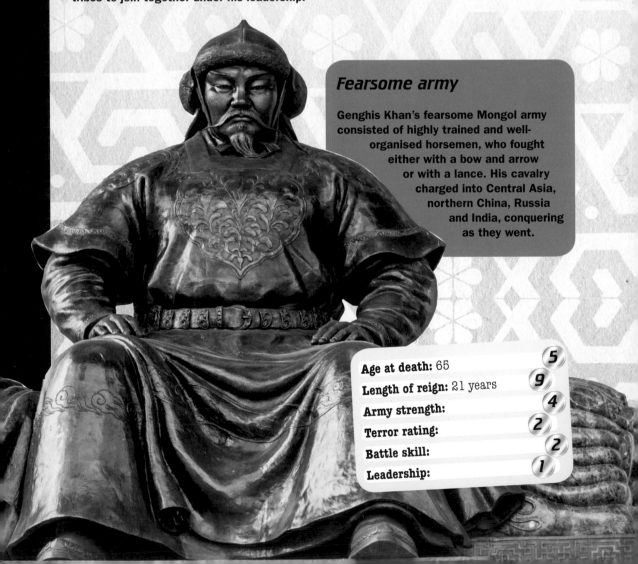

Fearsome army

Genghis Khan's fearsome Mongol army
consisted of highly trained and well-
organised horsemen, who fought
either with a bow and arrow
or with a lance. His cavalry
charged into Central Asia,
northern China, Russia
and India, conquering
as they went.

Age at death: 65	5
Length of reign: 21 years	9
Army strength:	4
Terror rating:	2
Battle skill:	2
Leadership:	1

Attila the Hun

Attila the Hun was leader of the most terrifying barbarian tribe of all, which conquered great chunks of the Roman Empire.

Age at death: 43 — **16**

Length of reign: 19 years — **11**

Army strength: — **6**

Terror rating: — **1**

Battle skill: — **5**

Leadership: — **14**

Barbarians

The Huns were nomads from Central Asia with a large empire. By the time Attila became King of the Huns in 434 CE, the Roman Empire had weakened and split in two. In the 440s they attacked the Eastern Roman Empire, but stopped when they got to the capital, Constantinople. In 453 he died – there's a story that he choked on a nosebleed on his wedding night, but he might have been murdered by a rival.

Destroying cities

Attila the Hun invaded Gaul but was driven out by the Romans. In revenge, he attacked the Western Roman Empire, where he destroyed the cities of Milan, Padua and Verona (among others).

Alexander the Great

Alexander the Great conquered most of the known world in just 12 years. During that time his mighty army was never defeated.

Ruthless ruler

Alexander became King of Macedonia, which ruled most of Greece, in 336 BCE. The city state of Thebes revolted against Alexander's bloodthirsty rule, so Alexander destroyed Thebes, killed thousands and sold everyone else as slaves – he was utterly ruthless.

Conquering Persia

Alexander's forces pushed into Persia, first in Asia Minor (now Turkey), then along the Mediterranean and in Egypt. He fought the Persian leader's army, won a decisive battle, and became King of Asia. Alexander went on to conquer Susa, the capital of Persia, and Babylon. He continued eastwards, determined to make his empire even bigger, and defeated an elephant-mounted Indian army. Alexander died in Babylon, after a huge party, aged 33. He had conquered most of the known world in just 12 years as king.

Age at death: 33

Length of reign: 13 years

Army strength:

Terror rating:

Battle skill:

Leadership:

19
14
1
3
1
4

Charlemagne

Charlemagne was a warrior king whose powerful empire lasted almost 1,000 years! He brought Christianity to large parts of Europe.

King of the Franks

The Franks' kingdom was mostly in what's now France. Charlemagne took over from his father as King of the Franks in 768 CE. Charlemagne waged a long and bloody war with the neighbouring kingdom of Saxony, but eventually he won. In 804, he forced the Saxons to become Christians.

Age at death: 71		2
Length of reign: 14 years		13
Army strength:		13
Terror rating:		17
Battle skill:		13
Leadership:		8

Emperor of Rome

During the war with the Saxons, the Pope asked Charlemagne to help fight the Lombards – who weren't Catholic. Charlemagne defeated them, and continued conquering into what's now Germany and Austria. He made the people he'd conquered convert to Christianity. In 800, while the Frankish empire grew, the Pope crowned Charlemagne Emperor of the Romans. Charlemagne's empire later became known as the Holy Roman Empire, and lasted until 1806.

Qin Shi Huang

In 246 BCE, Qin Shi Huang became King of Qin – one of the seven Chinese states. He went on to become China's first emperor in 221 BCE – and had an entire terracotta army built for his tomb.

United China

Qin Shi Huang (as he was known later, meaning 'first emperor') attacked each of the six other states in China. It took nine years for him to conquer them all: he now ruled the whole of China. During his reign invaders became a problem in the north, so Qin Shi Huang built a wall to keep them out – an early version of the Great Wall of China. He ordered books to be burnt unless they were about particular subjects, and executed people for reading forbidden books.

Terracotta army

Qin Shi Huang made himself what is probably the most impressive tomb ever: a vast underground chamber guarded by thousands of life-size warriors and horses made of terracotta. The tomb was discovered by accident in the 1970s, and so far more than 7,000 figures have been unearthed. Qin Shi Huang was buried inside his tomb in 210 BCE.

Age at death: 49 — **14**
Length of reign: 11 years — **15**
Army strength: **11**
Terror rating: **9**
Battle skill: **13**
Leadership: **6**

Napoleon Bonaparte

Napoleon Bonaparte became a hero during the French Revolution (1789–1799). After he led an attack against a royalist rebellion and saved the day, Napoleon was given command of the French revolutionary army – even though he'd been just an ordinary artillery officer. Later, he seized power and became Emperor of France.

Victory and defeat

Authorities in many countries in Europe wanted an end to the French Revolution. They were worried that radical ideas might spread, and during the French Revolution lots of French aristocrats had their heads chopped off! Napoleon led the French to victories against the Austrians and Italians, but suffered defeat too. He invaded Russia in 1812 but was forced to retreat, and hundreds of thousands of his men died. France was forced to surrender.

Battle of Waterloo

Napoleon went into exile, but made a comeback in 1815. He rallied a new French army to face the combined forces of Britain, Russia, Prussia and Austria, but at the Battle of Waterloo he was defeated again.

Age at death: 51 — 13

Length of reign: 11 years — 15

Army strength: — 15

Terror rating: — 17

Battle skill: — 13

Leadership: — 15

Julius Caesar

Julius Caesar gained a powerful position in the republic of ancient Rome, which was ruled by elected leaders called Consuls. He began his conquering as governor of Spain, invading Portugal and winning land and riches for Rome.

Age at death: 55   **11**

Length of reign: 5 years   **17**

Army strength: **3**

Terror rating: **16**

Battle skill: **4**

Leadership: **16**

Ruler of Rome

Caesar was made Consul of Rome, but then seized control of Rome with two other Roman generals, Crassus and Pompey. Caesar began the Gallic Wars and, after seven years' fighting, added modern-day France and Belgium to the Roman Empire. Caesar went to war with Pompey after Crassus died, defeated him and made himself Dictator of the Roman Empire for ten years. Then he went a step further: in 44 BCE he made himself Dictator for Life. This upset the politicians who wanted Rome to remain a republic (without a king or queen). They assassinated Caesar – he was stabbed and killed by 23 of them.

William the Conqueror

William of Normandy was a French duke who invaded England after Harold Godwinson took the throne. William's most famous victory was at the Battle of Hastings.

Duke of Normandy

William had been Duke of Normandy since about the age of seven. His cousin, Edward the Confessor, was King of England, and William said that Edward had named him as his heir to the throne. But when Edward died, a Saxon called Harold Godwinson was made King of England instead.

Battle of Hastings

William decided to invade: he gathered an army and landed on the south coast of England, and began attacking English towns. King Harold had to fight a battle in the north of England, then marched south to meet William. At the Battle of Hastings, William defeated Harold's army. He was crowned King of England on Christmas Day 1066, and the Normans took over the country. William ruled for twenty-one years, until he died in 1087.

Age at death: 59 — 7

Length of reign: 21 years — 9

Army strength: — 10

Terror rating: — 20

Battle skill: — 18

Leadership: — 13

Cyrus the Great

Cyrus was King of the Persians (in modern-day Iran) and went on to create the First Persian Empire in the 6th century BCE. At the time, it was the largest empire ever known.

Conquering career

Cyrus began his conquering career by overthrowing the Medes, who ruled the kingdom, and uniting them with the Persians. Cyrus expanded his empire, conquering Asia Minor (now Turkey) and then the Babylonian Empire. Eventually his empire, known as the First Persian Empire or the Achaemenid Empire, stretched from the Mediterranean Sea to the Indus River.

Wise ruler

Cyrus was a great conqueror, but he also ruled wisely, efficiently and justly. He was tolerant of all religions – for example, he allowed the Jewish captives in Babylon to return to their homeland – and drew up the first ever human rights charter. After Cyrus died, his empire lasted more than two centuries.

Age at death: 46   **18**

Length of reign: 29 years   **8**

Army strength: **7**

Terror rating: **19**

Battle skill: **9**

Leadership: **2**

Babur

Babur became ruler of Farghana (now part of Uzbekistan) when he was just 12 years old. You might say that conquering was in his blood — he was a descendant of both Genghis Khan and Tamurlane! Babur went on to found an empire of his own: the Mughul Empire in India.

Winning and losing

Two years after becoming king, Babur took the city of Samarkand, but then lost it again, along with Farghana. In 1504, he'd formed a new army and captured the city of Kabul, gaining a large and wealthy kingdom. Babur had to fight to keep it, especially against the fearsome Uzbeks.

Indian empire

Babur had been making raids into India since 1519. In 1526 he marched against the Sultan of Delhi and defeated him at the Battle of Panipat, even though Babur was heavily outnumbered. He went on to conquer an empire that encompassed most of northern India, with its capital at Agra. His son and grandson made the Mughul Empire bigger still.

Age at death: 47
Length of reign: 4 years
Army strength: 16
Terror rating: 18
Battle skill: 11
Leadership: 11

6

16

Sargon the Great

Sargon the Great was the world's first ever conquering emperor. He began as an important member at the court of the King of Kish, before becoming king himself — the story has been lost, so no one knows exactly how. Sargon ruled the Akkadian Empire more than 4,000 years ago.

Age at death: Unknown — **11**

Length of reign: c. 55 years — **1**

Army strength: **7**

Terror rating: **4**

Battle skill: **11**

Leadership: **8**

Akkadian Empire

Sargon quickly began attacking and capturing other cities and regions, and soon he was in control of the whole of Sumer (now southern Iraq, where the first ever civilisation began). Sargon ruled from his capital city, Akkad, and his language, Akkadian, became the official language of the empire.

Expanded empire

After he became king, Sargon expanded his empire so that it stretched from the Mediterranean to the Persian Gulf, including some of what's now Iran, Iraq and Turkey. Today, no one knows where the city of Akkad used to stand. The empire of Sargon the Great lasted for another 150 years after he died, until around 2129 BCE.

Hernán Cortés

Spanish conquistador Hernán Cortés sailed to the Americas to make his fortune. After helping to conquer Cuba, Hernando set off for Mexico in 1519, which had recently been "discovered" by Europeans.

Montezuma's Mexico

Mexico was ruled by Montezuma II, Emperor of the Aztecs. Cortés took Montezuma hostage and demanded a ransom from the Aztecs. An Aztec revolt, in which Montezuma died, drove Cortés out, but he returned and captured the capital city — Tenochtitlan. Cortés built Mexico City on the ruins and Spanish colonists settled there. Eventually, after some more exploring, he returned to Spain, where he died.

Age at death: 62	**6**
Length of reign: n/a	**20**
Army strength:	**20**
Terror rating:	**6**
Battle skill:	**19**
Leadership:	**19**

Awful for Aztecs

Cortés ruled cruelly over the Aztecs as Governor and Captain General of New Spain. The Aztec people were almost wiped out by diseases from Europe, such as smallpox, and because of their poor treatment.

Mahmud of Ghazni

Mahmud became ruler of the Ghaznavid kingdom (modern-day Afghanistan and northeastern Iran), in 998 CE. He began expanding his kingdom straight away, marching westwards, and capturing more land.

Invading India

In 1001, Mahmud made the first of many invasions of India. He pitted his strong cavalry against the fierce, elephant-mounted warriors of Rajput, and added chunks of northern India and what's now Pakistan to his empire.

Plundering

Mahmud made 17 invasions of India altogether. Each time he plundered the rich, fertile lands of northern India. He destroyed thousands of Hindu temples during his raids. At Somnath, 50,000 people died defending the temple. Later, Mahmud used the temple's golden doors as steps to a mosque in his capital at Kabul. By the time he died, Mahmud's empire included much of what's now Afghanistan, Uzbekistan, Turkmenistan, Kyrgyzstan, Pakistan and northern India.

Age at death: 59   **8**

Length of reign: 4 years   **18**

Army strength: **17**

Terror rating: **6**

Battle skill: **19**

Leadership: **11**

Mehmed II

Mehmed became Sultan of the Ottoman Empire in 1451, and quickly ordered a fortress and a fleet of ships to be built. He also ordered weapons, including bigger cannon — some were bigger than any ever seen before!

Roman conqueror

Mehmed used his new weapons to besiege the city of Constantinople (now called Istanbul), the capital of the Byzantine Empire, or Eastern Roman Empire. He captured Constantinople in 1453, absorbed the Byzantine Empire into the Ottoman Empire, and took the title "Caesar of Rome".

Keep on conquering

Mehmet led his army into Serbia, Bosnia, Greece and Anatolia (now part of Turkey). His greatest victory came in 1471 when he won the Battle of Bashkent and took control of Anatolia and the Balkans. He was still conquering when he died in 1481, having invaded Italy in an attempt to reunite the old Roman Empire. He left behind him a stronger and bigger Ottoman Empire than ever before.

Age at death: 49	**14**
Length of reign: 32 years (total)	**5**
Army strength:	**13**
Terror rating:	**11**
Battle skill:	**6**
Leadership:	**11**

Odoacer

Odoacer was a Germanic warrior who became a soldier in the Roman army. When the Romans refused to give the soldiers the land they had been promised, Odoacer led other soldiers in a rebellion.

Age at death: 58	9
Length of reign: 17 years	12
Army strength:	17
Terror rating:	11
Battle skill:	17
Leadership:	19

Rebel soldiers

Odoacer's rebel army defeated the Roman general Orestes in 476 CE. Emperor Romulus Augustus, Orestes's son, was quickly captured. Odoacer became the first barbarian (non-Roman) King of Italy, though he still acknowledged Byzantine Emperor Zeno. Later, Odoacer captured the island of Sicily from the Vandals, and conquered Dalmatia (now part of Croatia), while losing some of northern Italy to the Visigoths.

Odoacer's end

In 488, Theodoric, leader of the Ostrogoth tribe, was appointed King of Italy by Emperor Zeno. This was to stop the Ostrogoths from invading the Eastern Roman Empire. Theodoric invaded Italy and quickly took control of most of the country, and Odoacer was forced to retreat. Then Theodoric invited Odoacer to a banquet, where he killed him.

Thutmose III

Thutmose III was just two years old when his reign began in 1479 BCE. For the first 22 years his stepmother, Hatshepsut, ruled for him. When Hatshepsut died, Thutmose began to expand his empire.

Expanding empire

Thutmose's first major battle was against the King of Kadesh, in what's now Syria, who gathered an army against him at the time of Hatshepsut's death. Thutmose defeated the King of Kadesh, and during the following years conquered large chunks of Syria, the kingdom of Mitanni and southern Anatolia. He also conquered lands to the south of Egypt, in Nubia (modern-day Sudan).

Greatest pharaoh

Thutmose captured around 350 cities, and waged 17 campaigns in 20 years. He was such a fearsome conqueror that the kingdoms surrounding his empire sent gifts and tributes. For centuries after he was famous as the greatest Egyptian pharaoh.

Age at death: 56

Length of reign: 54 years

Army strength: 2

Terror rating: 2

Battle skill: 6

Leadership: 3

10

10

Zhu Yuanzhang

Born a peasant in 1328, Zhu Yuanzhang grew up in a time of drought, famine and plague. He joined others in rebellions against the rich. He was a skilled warrior and leader, and soon became head of a rebel army that captured towns and cities in the east of China, including Nanjing.

Peasant army

With a large army behind him, Zhu Yuanzhang (later called Hongwu, meaning 'huge force') was determined to overthrow the ruling Yuan (Mongol) Dynasty. He took control of southern China, and in 1368 proclaimed himself Emperor of the Ming Dynasty. After sending troops to fight the Mongols in the north, and capturing the Mongol capital city (modern-day Beijing), Zhu Yuanzhang had control of the whole of China by 1382. He later expanded his empire into Mongolia and Central Asia.

Ming Dynasty

The Ming Dynasty ruled China until the mid-17th century. Throughout its history, the Ming Dynasty battled against the Mongols and other invaders from the north, and built a large chunk of the Great Wall of China to keep them out.

Age at death: 69

Length of reign: 30 years

Army strength:

Terror rating:

Battle skill:

Leadership:

3

7

4

14

15

5

King Piye

Piye was King of Kush, part of ancient Nubia or modern-day Sudan. Within the first ten years of his reign, he took control of Upper Egypt.

Age at death: 31	**20**
Length of reign: 29 years	**6**
Army strength:	**17**
Terror rating:	**5**
Battle skill:	**11**
Leadership:	**8**

Invasion force

Tefnakht, Prince of the kingdom of Sais, formed an alliance with the kings of the Nile Delta region against King Piye. Piye assembled a fearsome army ready to invade Middle and Lower Egypt. He marched against Tefnakht's alliance and won a decisive victory. He captured the cities of Herakliopolis, Hermopolis and Memphis, the ancient Egyptian capital.

Egyptian dynasty

Tefnakht fled, after conceding defeat, and the kings of the Nile Delta submitted and paid homage to King Piye. When Piye died, his brother Shabaka took full control of Egypt and became the first pharoah of the 25th Dynasty.

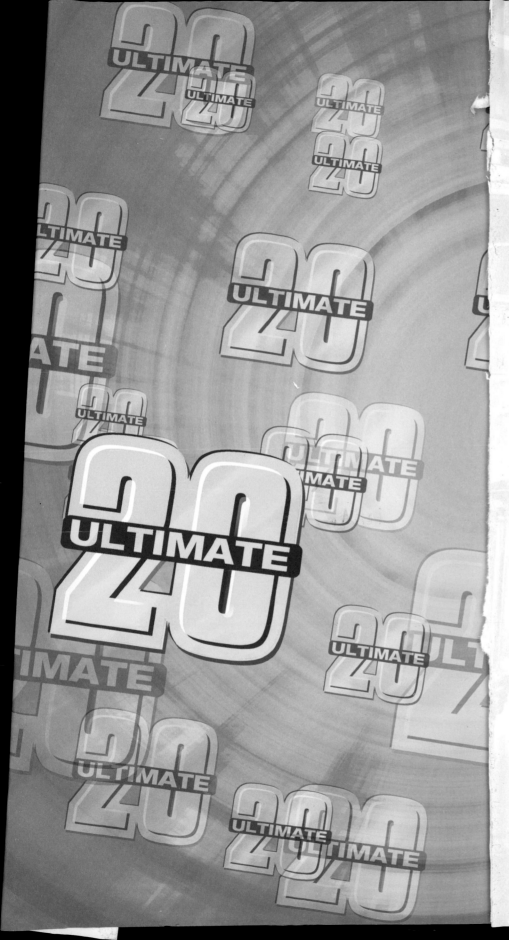

Glossary

Americas – refers to North and South America

Asia Minor – the area of Asia which is now modern Turkey

Aztecs – the people who controlled northern Mexico before Cortés invaded in the 16th century

Babylon – an ancient city on the River Euphrates, the remains of which are in Hillah, Iraq

barbarian – in Roman times, anyone who wasn't a Roman, Greek or Christian

BCE/CE – 'before the common era/common era' – it is used as a way of identifying historical dates

besiege – to surround a place, such as a castle or city, with armed forces in order to force it to surrender

cavalry – soldiers riding on horseback

Constantinople – a city now called Istanbul, in Turkey

empire – a large number of countries under the rule of a single country or emperor

human rights – basic rights and freedoms that should belong to every person

Lombards – people who lived in the area of modern Germany

Persia – the old name for Iran

pharaoh – the name for rulers in ancient Egypt

republic – a country or state that is ruled by elected representatives rather than by a king

terracotta – hard unglazed pottery

Index